Expressions From Lancashire

Edited by Claire Tupholme & Helen Davies

First published in Great Britain in 2010 by

 Young**Writers**

Remus House
Coltsfoot Drive
Peterborough
PE2 9JX
Telephone: 01733 890066
Website: www.youngwriters.co.uk

Foreword

At Young Writers our defining aim is to promote an enjoyment of reading and writing amongst children and young adults. By giving aspiring poets the opportunity to see their work in print, their love of the written word as well as confidence in their own abilities has the chance to blossom.

Our latest competition Poetry Explorers was designed to introduce primary school children to the wonders of creative expression. They were given free reign to write on any theme and in any style, thus encouraging them to use and explore a variety of different poetic forms.

We are proud to present the resulting collection of regional anthologies which are an excellent showcase of young writing talent. With such a diverse range of entries received, the selection process was difficult yet very rewarding. From comical rhymes to poignant verses, there is plenty to entertain and inspire within these pages. We hope you agree that this collection bursting with imagination is one to treasure.

Contents

Millbrook CP School

Queen's Drive Primary School

St Anne's CE Primary School, Wigan

St Anne's RC Primary School, Blackburn

St Bernadette's RC Primary School, Lancaster

St Mary's CE Primary School, Rochdale

St Peter's CE Primary School, Rochdale

Trinity & St Michael's CE School

The Poems

Go To Bed

'Go to bed,' Mum said.
'No I don't want to sleep,
I want to stay up
And on my feet.'

And this is my bedtime tale,
I dream of dragons,
Fierce and mean
With dark green scales
That will make you scream.

I climb the ridged rocks,
Up really, really high,
My quest is to seek
The midnight sky.

Catherine Brogna (11)
Brunshaw Primary School

Lunchtime

I'm carrying my lunch box, as heavy as can be
I wonder what's inside? I think, *maybe a surprise for me?*

I'm sitting in the dinner hall, right next to Betty Ball,
She looks at me curiously, I wonder why that could be?

So here I am sitting to have my lunch
An apple, a pear and a Munch Bunch
'Oh no, not this!' I say, 'it's exactly what I had yesterday!'

I give a big sigh, but then something meets my eye
All wrapped up like Blackpool rock, guess what?
It's my missing Jenga blocks!

You're probably wondering what's happened to me
I have two naughty brothers you see
It's just a silly trick they've played on me
Don't worry, I'll get them back at tea!

Hana Ibrahim (9)
Clarendon Primary School

My Mum Is The Sweetest

My mum is the sweetest
I love her very much
But sometimes she gets angry
Which makes me want to puff!

My mum is very special
Special as special as can be
And when I get upset
She's there to hug me.

My mum isn't perfect
But she's perfect enough for me
And when I see her
It gives me joy and happiness.

My mum isn't just a mother
But an angel sent from Heaven
And she's always on my mind
Even when she's in Devon.

Maryam Patel (9)
Clarendon Primary School

The Policeman

He is a stopper
A mighty crime copper.

He's a problem solver
A crime involver.

That's the job
It's got to be solved.

He doesn't let anyone get on his nerves
Especially if it's a nurse.

He caught the crook
Who stole the book!

Suleman Ahmed (9)
Clarendon Primary School

Monday Morning

'Time for school!' shouts Mum.
Oh no, has Monday come and the weekend gone?
Quick, quick, out of bed
'What's for breakfast?'
'Weetabix,' she says
Slowly down the stairs I go
Open my eyes then open the door
Gulp my breakfast down and watch the clock go tick
'Come on, let's be quick!'
Upstairs to brush my teeth and wash my face
Let's see, where is my pencil case?
School bag packed and brush my hair
Why school today? It's just not fair!
Off to school we walk
Gives me and Dad some time to talk
I see my friends at the school gate
I love school, it's just great!

Razeenah Ougradar (7)
Clarendon Primary School

Gloomy Classrooms!

At the front of the classroom there's a teacher
Waving a big battered beater
She points at the big blackboard
That rolls down on a cord
And the children are sitting in rows
Who are very bored.

Tempted to look outside
Which they cannot abide
A boy called Jake
He eats too much cake
He comes to the classroom with a stomach ache.

Would you like to be in a gloomy classroom?

Aaminah Seedat (9)
Clarendon Primary School

The School Day

We're off to school, my sister and I
To my mummy and daddy I say goodbye.

I run to my classroom, it's time for registration
Next it's addition, subtraction, multiplication.

On go our PE kits, into the hall we go
I hope it's not beach ball, I find it such a bore.

Ring goes the bell, it's time for lunch
I wonder what my mum's given me to munch?

Back into my classroom, it's time to write
Even though I don't like it, I must do it right!

Painting and drumming is next on the list
I like it so much I don't want to miss.

Ring goes the bell, it's hometime for me
I get in the car, I wonder what Mum's made for tea . . .

Amara Ibrahim (8)
Clarendon Primary School

What Is Your Special Day?

A birthday is always your special day
You always get your own way
Presents and cards are brought to you
And the girls always get a pretty hairdo.

When you're at school
People say you're cool
They crowd around you
As if you're new.

I am going to say something
I don't care who to
If it's your birthday today
Then happy birthday to you!

Aaisha Patel (10)
Clarendon Primary School

Waiting On The Corner

I'm waiting on the corner
In front of the shop door
I'm having a tantrum
To people that I don't know.

My parents are late
And the shopkeeper I hate
Is giving me some sweets
And calling me Pete!

It is night-time
And I'm eating lime
I can hear a noise
But it's just some boys.

Oh dear
My parents are not here!

Aishah Asjid (9)
Clarendon Primary School

Coca-Cola Lover's Confession

Coca-Cola, Coca-Cola
How I love my beautiful Coca-Cola
Coke in the day
Coke in the night
I'll never let it out of sight
Loving it more than treasure
In the world
I will never let it have a swirl
And did you know
For a fact
I drank so much Coke at work
That I got sacked?
I still love my phenomenal Coke
So don't you forget that my little folk!

Aisha Muslam (10)
Clarendon Primary School

Teachers

Without a teacher you would not learn
Your mind would start to burn
With questions, with unknown answers
Like sums and spellings and scientific answers
In maths there's decimals and fractions
The teacher teaches us weird actions
Literacy's boring and poems are fun
Today's snack was a hot-crossed bun
So what do you think about school?

Amna Wajid (10)
Clarendon Primary School

Racism

Racism is bad
It makes everyone sad
It hurts their feelings
When everyone's teasing
It's bad calling them names
Hang your head in shame
Would you like it if it happened to you?
Would you feel happy or in the blue?

Afsana Hassan (9)
Clarendon Primary School

Jelly Belly

Oh, I love scrummy, yummy jelly
Oh, if it is very cold when it goes in my belly
It would be silly and smelly
If I put it in my welly
Oh, it is best to keep it in my belly
Oh, I love scrummy, yummy jelly!

Nadia Lakdawala (7)
Clarendon Primary School

I Wish

I wish the world was bright
Filled with lots of light
My heart is full of smiles
Which will last me for miles
The world is full of happiness
Because of all the magicness
It is now the end of May
So say goodbye to the 31 days.

Usamah Muhammad (9)
Clarendon Primary School

The Wiggly Worm

Little, little worm, wiggle, wiggle, wiggle
You make my brothers and sisters giggle, giggle, giggle.
You live in lots of mud
And have lots of love
Thank you little worm
Wiggle, wiggle, wiggle.

Amina Muslam (10)
Clarendon Primary School

Love

Love is red like a lovely garden of red roses
Love smells like a red, red, fairy rose
Love is so sweet like squishy red lips
Love is so cuddly like a pink loving bear
Love is kind and trusting like a lovely princess
Love reminds me of a red fairy horse.

Fatima Amin (8)
Hawthorns Junior School

Happiness

Happiness is like a frog leaping across lily pads
To the other side of the pond
Happiness is a golden sunflower swaying in the breeze
Happiness spreads like the sun's golden rays across the Earth
Happiness is like the nesting birds singing sweetly in the great oak
trees.

Hashim Ismail (8)
Hawthorns Junior School

Love

Love is red like a bunch of red flowers in the nice bright sky
Love is sweet like sticky pink candyfloss
Love feels smooth and soft like a cute newborn baby
Love sounds calm when a mother's singing a lullaby to her baby
Love reminds me of my loving and caring family.

Aneesha Baig (8)
Hawthorns Junior School

Peace

Peace is fluffy like candyfloss
Peace is the birds humming through the wintry breeze
Peace is green like two white doves on a tree
Peace is pure lavender like drifting through the night air
Peace is the moon and the stars shining up in the dark sky.

Maariyah Peeru (9)
Hawthorns Junior School

Happiness

Happiness is bright like the beaming sun
Happiness smells of swaying daffodils dancing in the velvety sky
Happiness sounds like a room full of laughter
Happiness is dancing in my heart
Happiness reminds me of my mother when she makes lovely food.

Hamza Shazad (8)
Hawthorns Junior School

Sleep

Sleep is like you are moving on a peaceful blue sea
Sleep smells like pure lavender
Sleeps feels calm, smooth and comfortable
Sleep looks like a snoozing cat curled up in front of an open fire.

Israr Hussain (9)
Hawthorns Junior School

Sleep

Sleep sounds peaceful like a baby sleeping in its cot.
Sleep is like a great cuddle from your comfy teddy bear.
Sleep reminds me of my dreams coming true in the moonlight.
Sleep is like a blushing of clouds on a great summer's day.

Mehak Shah (9)
Hawthorns Junior School

Dylan

D is for deadly assassin
Y is for young and cool
L is for Liverpool
A is for awesome Arsenal
N is for Ninja warrior.

Dylan Hughes (8)
Holy Cross CE (VA) Primary School

The Haunted House

Spooky, a deserted house alone.
Lighting struck - all you could hear was groaning.
Snap, snap, snap, a branch came off the tree and ended up at the
top of the house
I heard a crackling noise on the roof
But it was just a branch crushing something, it was a tooth.
A creak came from the house, it smelled vile, it was a cat.
Then I heard a squeak, it was a mouse.
Down, down, down, all you heard was a piece of floorboard as it
went downstairs.
As a cat came downstairs all I saw was a foot - who was up there?
Did they live there?

Jessica Campbell (10)
Holy Cross CE (VA) Primary School

Haunted House

Lightning strikes, the creepy gnarled trees surrounding the deserted
house.
Shabby windows reflect the familiar moonlight.
The house scares away the animals
With its awful odour, so now it's quiet as a mouse.
The chimney is as rusty as an old bike, really gives people a fright.
As solid as can be the door slams shut.
Ivy as smooth as a sheep quickly climbs the walls.
This house is the most terrible house in the whole world
It is really a hut
Pebbles as crunchy as a boat, pebbles crunch under your feet.

Ellie McGuirk (10)
Holy Cross CE (VA) Primary School

Roxy And I

Roxy and I play like we should
We leap together, sleep together
Explore together, play together
Shop together, hop together
Laugh together, eat together
Cook together, tidy together
Shine together, fly together
Travel together, try together
Dance together, prance together
Learn together
We do everything together.

Sophie Pickering (9)
Holy Cross CE (VA) Primary School

I Like To Run, It Makes Me So Strong

I like to run, you get so strong
I also like to exercise
You get so fit
I like to play
It makes me so happy
I like to play football as well
Because you get a prize
And I like to read
Because you get smart!

Juher Ahmed (7)
Holy Cross CE (VA) Primary School

My Feet Walk

I can stamp my feet
I can wiggle my toes
I can jump with my feet
I can tickle my toes
I can kick with my feet
I can bounce on my toes
I can skip with my feet
I can wiggle my feet
My feet sleep
My feet are tired.

Bethany Mairs (8)
Holy Cross CE (VA) Primary School

How My Feet Work

I can wiggle my toes
I can wiggle my toes
I can run very fast
But I never come last
I can walk very slowly
Then I always come last
I can run very fast
No one knows
I can walk very fast
But then my legs get tired.

Shamima Begum (8)
Holy Cross CE (VA) Primary School

My School

The school is very nice
The teachers are nice too
This place is the best school ever
In the whole universe.

Mohamed Bary (8)
Holy Cross CE (VA) Primary School

Abdullah - More Than A Name

A is for active, so full of fun
B is for beloved, everyone's friend
D is for dependable, on me you can rely
U is for unique, a very special son
L is for life, that you live so well
L is for lively, so full of imagination
A is for alive, clever and bright
H is for honest, cheerful and smiley.

Abdullah is much more than just a name!

Abdullah Al-Mamoun (10)
Holy Cross CE (VA) Primary School

Holy Cross

H is for the Holy Bible
O is for opportunity
L is to like each other
Y is for young children, who I help

C is for parish church
R is for ruling the school
O is for Oldham
S is for smiling in school
S is for sharing with each other.

Rahima Khatun (8)
Holy Cross CE (VA) Primary School

Words About Mason

M arvellous
A wesome
S uper
O utstanding
N inja warrior.

Mason Rodney Julien (8)
Holy Cross CE (VA) Primary School

Haunted House!

Horrifying house standing there tall, appears to be abandoned.
Moonlight glistening bright on the broken glass windows that are creaking.
Shivering with horror and terror, nobody knows what really happened.
Passengers wondering if they heard dripping and leaking.
Villagers shivering with fear wondering what's making them do that.
Snap! Down comes a branch on the damp, disastrous ground.
Thunder cracking in the night sky like a bat.
Sizzling thunder going round and round.

Sadia Rahman (10)
Holy Cross CE (VA) Primary School

The Creaky House

Bang! The old grave door slams shut.
Boom! The thunder crashed like stones
Crash! The large branch broken in bits.
Crackle! Then falling to pieces.
Creak! The floor creaking in bits.
Snap! The leaves when the cat goes past.
Smash! The windows smash in pieces.
Puff! The smoky chimney flames.

Gabby Ramsbottom (10)
Holy Cross CE (VA) Primary School

My Heart

My heart each and every time
My heart beats all the time
It never ever stops beating
My heart beats when I do something
When I skip or hop it beats
When I am in bed
I can feel my heart beating.

Masnuna Chowdhury
Holy Cross CE (VA) Primary School

My Heart

My heart is light red
It beats when I'm in bed
My heart never stops
My heart will not pop
My heart is the best
It never helps me in a test
My heart is as big as my fist
My heart will always resist.

Brendan Hammond (7)
Holy Cross CE (VA) Primary School

Spooky House

Bang! The spooky door slams shut.
Boom! The strange thunder and lightning in the sky.
Crash! The large big branch fell on top of the green grass,
Crackle! The hard rocks cracked under the soft ground.
Creak! The smoke glitters round the house in a burning smell.
Snap! The green grass glitters in front of the house.
Smash! The house is old and disgusting.
Puff! I can smell smoke in the garage.

Cynthia Ajong Sinju (10)
Holy Cross CE (VA) Primary School

The Spooky Haunted House

Bang! The trees fell on the ground
The lightning made a huge sound
Smoke as blurry as fog drifted along the air
It seemed that the spooky house was always bare
The haunted house always looked frightening
I jumped out of my skin when I heard lightning
The green, creepy ivy climbed up the wall
The terrifying, abandoned house always stands tall.

Shumon Miah (10)
Holy Cross CE (VA) Primary School

Lungs

We have two gigantic juicy lungs
They puff and puff when we rush
Our lungs puff like balloons
Our wobbly lungs dance when we dance as well
When we puff out, our lungs go like a balloon's air coming out
My lungs dance with my heart
They always bounce when they fight
The lungs are squashed.

Sadiya Chowdry
Holy Cross CE (VA) Primary School

Autumn

Autumn leaves are falling down gently, smothering the ground
Never going speedily down
Going down to make it bare
Through the night the leaves fall down
Trees are glimmering and shining
Till they scramble through the day
They are beautiful, glimmering, shining
But you just glimmer just like me.

Rohima Begum (8)
Holy Cross CE (VA) Primary School

School

S is for smile
C is for caring
H is for happy
O is for optional work
O is for organised school
L is for learning well

I love school.

Nazmin Begum (8)
Holy Cross CE (VA) Primary School

The Name Poem

R is for ridiculous when the teacher says that's not right
A is for alphabet where you learn letters from
H is for hungry when people want to eat food
I is for imagine when people want to have something for teal
M is for memory but I don't know what it means
U is for ugly when this boy can be ugly
R is for reminder because remember to say to me, bye-bye!

Rahimur Rahman (8)
Holy Cross CE (VA) Primary School

Autumn

A utumn leaves are falling down, red, brown and green
U p and down, up and down, up and down with multicoloured,
wonderful leaves
T he leaves are crunchy, crunchy, yum-yum-yum
U p the trees are cuddly leaves, red, brown, green and yellow
M ight you go to bed tonight you might just get a fright
N oisy night-time bugs come alive at night.

Jahid Miah (8)
Holy Cross CE (VA) Primary School

Snow Poem

Snow is fluffy, snow is fun
Snow is cold, it freezes my nose
Snow comes in winter
Down from the sky
It goes away in spring
And it comes in winter
All over again.

Sunia Begum (8)
Holy Cross CE (VA) Primary School

Spooksville

S trange, spooky silence! There is old ivy climbing the walls.
P etrified calls come screaming out of the abandoned, rotten land.
O ddly-shaped trees protect the house with their rough hands.
O dours come out of the house and turn beautiful mice yellow.
K een to keep going, the ivy reaches the top of the mouldy house.
Y ells of horror scare people away. The scary, twisted house
   has been empty until this day.

Chloe McFaul (10)
Holy Cross CE (VA) Primary School

Autumn

A utumn leaves are falling down
U p in the tree leaves are orange and brown
T wirling around in the lovely breeze
U p above the leaves are turning
M agical leaves floating around
N ice crunchy leaves on the ground.

Ami Moss (8)
Holy Cross CE (VA) Primary School

Autumn

A utumn leaves are falling down
U p in the tree there are loads of leaves
T he leaves are falling down
U p the tree there are loads of leaves
M ulticoloured leaves are up in the trees
N ice leaves are up in the trees.

Liam Becsby (8)
Holy Cross CE (VA) Primary School

Autumn

A utumn leaves are falling down to meet their friends
U p and down the leaves are flowing around
T he leaves are curling up and down
U p above the leaves are swirling
M ulticoloured leaves are up in the trees
N eat leaves are up in the trees.

Saffryon Hague (8)
Holy Cross CE (VA) Primary School

Autumn

A ll the leaves are falling down gently
U p and down sparkling on the ground
T rees are so unusual and bare
U nder the trees you will find the hidden, magnificent leaves
M oment you step on them they begin to talk, *crunch, crunch*
N ice and calm.

Arooj Fatima (8)
Holy Cross CE (VA) Primary School

Autumn

A ll the leaves are falling down
U p and down the trees
T he leaves crunch and sway
U sing their crunch to make sounds
M ost leaves crunch
N ice, nice, the leaves crunch.

Alisha Ali Ruma (8)
Holy Cross CE (VA) Primary School

Autumn

A ll the leaves are falling down
U p and down the leaves are swooping down
T wirling down, floating around
U sually all shiny leaves fall down
M ighty leaves fall down out of the trees
N ice leaves twirl down.

Bethany Beirlerly (8)
Holy Cross CE (VA) Primary School

Autumn

A utumn leaves are falling down
U p and down they flow around
T ipple and turn, they stay down
U sing their crunch to make a sound
M oving, twirling, crunching, curling
N ice and crunchy for the ground.

Caitlin Eve Fox (8)
Holy Cross CE (VA) Primary School

All About Bones

We have 206 bones in our bodies
They wiggle and giggle about in my body
They dance around in my body
Some of my bones break
My bones, my bones
I like my bones.

Alima Khatun
Holy Cross CE (VA) Primary School

Autumn

A ll the leaves are falling down
U p and down they always go
T rees have got them
U nder the trees they go
M ulticoloured here we come
N ice and crunchy.

Michael Shenton (8)
Holy Cross CE (VA) Primary School

Autumn

A utumn leaves are falling down to the ground
U nderground the badgers collect food
T rees stand bare in the wind
U se the leaves to make art
M ysterious noises come out at night
N ight-time bugs might give you a fright.

Kane Lee Hall (9)
Holy Cross CE (VA) Primary School

Bouncing Thai Boxer

B ouncing Thai boxer
A wesome runner
E xciting video gamer
L oves Italian food
E nergetic schoolboy
I s really cool!

Baelei O'Rourke (8)
Holy Cross CE (VA) Primary School

Autumn

A ll over the floor are crunchy leaves
U pon the trees there are beautiful leaves
T he trees are getting all cold because the leaves are all gone
U nder the trees there are crunchy leaves
M unchy, munchy, beautiful leaves
N ow there are beautiful leaves.

Asia Akhtar (9)
Holy Cross CE (VA) Primary School

Autumn

A pples growing on the trees
U p in the trees the leaves are brown
T he leaves are falling down and down
U ntil they reach the ground
M isty mornings, cold and damp
N ovember night-time, chilly and dark.

Nafla Akran & Sumaiyah Ul Husna (8)
Holy Cross CE (VA) Primary School

Autumn

A utumn leaves are falling down
U p in the tree leaves are falling
T wirling down the tree
U p above the leaves are turning
M umbling around
N ice and crunchy.

Khira Wood (8)
Holy Cross CE (VA) Primary School

Autumn

A ll the leaves are falling down
U nder the trees are crunchy leaves
T he trees are beautiful and bold
U p in the trees there are no leaves
M ild weather, cold or warm
N ice, crumbly, crunchy leaves fall again.

Jack North (8)
Holy Cross CE (VA) Primary School

My Name Is Kia, So Cool!

My name is Kia
I like tools
Love school
But most of all
I am quite cool!

Kia Angus (8)
Holy Cross CE (VA) Primary School

Happiness

Happiness is going to Hyndburn Park Primary School
Happiness is getting a new pet cat
Happiness is having a birthday party
Happiness is playing games at home
Happiness is doing painting in class
Happiness is reading a story book
Happiness is feeding the squirrels in autumn
Happiness is working in school to learn
Happiness is looking at the fish
Happiness is listening to the birds sing
Happiness is going to the zoo
Happiness is having a new house
Happiness is having best friends.

Faiza Ahmed (8)
Hyndburn Park Primary School

Happiness

Happiness is having loads of lovely aunties and uncles
And two beautiful cute, cuddly cousins
Happiness is sitting in my uncle's black, shiny Audi
Happiness is going to school to learn
Happiness is having two lovely friends like Zainab and Aleema
Happiness is having loads of homework
Happiness is learning French
Happiness is celebrating Eid and eating sweets, samosas and kebabs
Happiness is having two courteous teachers like Mrs Raw and Miss Dixon
Happiness is sitting in the sun
Happiness is playing on my Nintendo DS
Happiness is when I go to my grandma's house or my aunts' houses
Happiness is a day at Blackpool
Happiness is watching a movie at the cinema
Happiness is a trip to the sports centre.

Aliyah Hussain (8)
Hyndburn Park Primary School

Happiness

Happiness is sitting in my uncle's shiny black car eating a fruity ice lolly
Happiness is doing exercise
Happiness is celebrating Eid and eating lots of delicious food
Happiness is eating chocolate cake
Happiness is going swimming
Happiness is playing football
Happiness is getting presents
Happiness is going to Blackpool
Happiness is going to Camelot
Happiness is getting a picture taken with my hair spiked up.

Usmaan Shakil (8)
Hyndburn Park Primary School

What I Like Or Dislike

I like butter, but the butter's bitter
So I decided to get new lovely butter.
I like smelling pancakes
But I hate it when horrible cheese is on them.
I like touching beautiful roses
But when I pick them I see a statue.
I like it when the sun comes out
Because you can eat lovely fresh ice cream.
I like it when it rains
Because you can hear the rain dripping.
I like playing with sand because you can go to a new land.
I like running, after that I will be tumbling.
I like to watch the moon when it goes behind the cloud
Then I see a balloon.
I like the colour red but I have to go to bed.
I don't like fools but I am cool.
I don't like the colour pink but I like to blink.

Haddiqa Nadeem (8)
Hyndburn Park Primary School

Happiness

Happiness is swimming at the sports centre
Happiness is playing outside
Happiness is doing art
Happiness is walking to school
Happiness is getting presents
Happiness is running
Happiness is being kind
Happiness is riding my bike
Happiness is seeing a film at the cinema
Happiness is drawing
Happiness is playing cricket.

Shiham Sahail (8)
Hyndburn Park Primary School

Happiness

Happiness is having servants to do jobs for you
Happiness is going to an interesting museum
Happiness is collecting conkers from the park
Happiness is playing out in the sunshine
Happiness is riding a shiny bike
Happiness is playing on a sunny beach
Happiness is doing French at school
Happiness is looking at different coloured leaves
Happiness is going to the Trafford Centre
Happiness is painting at school
Happiness is getting a PlayStation 2
Happiness is when it snows outside
Happiness is watching films at home
Happiness is testing projects at school
Happiness is playing kick rounders
Happiness is travelling to different places
Happiness is looking at the fireworks on Bonfire Night.

Saarah Parveen (8)
Hyndburn Park Primary School

Happiness

Happiness is getting a new shining Audi
Happiness is watching The Bill
Happiness is getting a good scooter
Happiness is having a takeaway
Happiness is going to school
Happiness is staying home
Happiness is getting sweets
Happiness is going to the fair
Happiness is playing dodgeball
Happiness is colouring.

Zakariya Khan (8)
Hyndburn Park Primary School

My Happy Days

I like playing PSP
I like eating pancakes
I like doing the talent show
I like Sunday swimming
I like sticking magnets on my fridge
I like counting colours on a rainbow
I like playing with play toys
I like stroking cute cats
I like mendie patterns on my hand
I like listening to Girls Aloud songs
I like playing with friends
I like sharpening pencils and pencil crayons
I like miaowing at my baby kitten
I like playing in the garden
I don't like school, it's very boring
I like eating packed lunch at school.

Zoya Ahmed (8)
Hyndburn Park Primary School

Happiness

Happiness is visiting my cousins
Happiness is rooting through my dad's garage
Happiness is eating jam doughnuts
Happiness is having tea at McDonald's, yum
Happiness is hugging my mum and dad
Happiness is going to Gatty Park
Happiness is getting a DKNY bag
Happiness is borrowing my sister's perfume
Happiness is learning in school
Happiness is looking at Mother Nature
Happiness is getting new stuff
Happiness is playing with my conkers
Happiness makes the world a beautiful place
And I am happy that I live in such a world.

Fyza Tariq (8)
Hyndburn Park Primary School

What I Like And Hate

I like writing with pens on rainbow paper
I like watching TV especially when Horrid Henry comes on
I like walking on laminated floor with high heels,
I always act like a teacher
I like Aligator Aliens, only green ones that are cute
I like crisps, salt and vinegar, sometimes McCoys
I like sweets, gooey, scrumptious ones
Sometimes my mum says no
I hate playing football
I hate Coke
I hate playing with babies, teddy bears, especially my brother
I hate people bossing other people, especially when they do it to me
I hate people that steal, well in school the most
I hate mints, I hate it when my sister says, 'Mmmm!'
When she eats them.

Zara Mahmood (8)
Hyndburn Park Primary School

Using My Senses

I like zooming through the windy trees
And then racing as fast as a cheetah

I like seeing buzzy bees
Imagining me as a buzzing bee

I like fighting through the forest winds
While jumping up and down

I like hearing the pouring rain
Imagining me having a dream

I like listening to Akon sing
And he is so awesome

I like songs, they are exciting
They are as musical as an instrument.

Muhammad Iqbal (8)
Hyndburn Park Primary School

Happiness

Happiness is shopping in the mall
Happiness is playing outside
Happiness is looking at pretty flowers
Happiness is learning different languages
Happiness is going to Blackpool
Happiness is playing with my friends
Happiness is being on the school council twice
Happiness is seeing my uncle, my best uncle
Happiness is having great joyful fun.

Zainab Ali (8)
Hyndburn Park Primary School

Happiness

Happiness is eating an ice lolly
Happiness is going to Year 4
Happiness is shopping in Blackburn
Happiness is having a picnic
Happiness is getting new stuff
Happiness is sitting in the sun
Happiness is doing art
Happiness is going to school
Happiness is going swimming.

Sanna Nazakat (8)
Hyndburn Park Primary School

Using My Senses

I like smelling rice, it is really nice.
I like watching the sun, it is really good fun.
I like walking to the park. when it is really dark.
I like touching bluebells, they are blue like the sky.
I like watching my friends happy like a lark.
I like listening to people laugh.

Rabia Waqar (8)
Hyndburn Park Primary School

My Senses

I like smelling bread, I like to spread onto my bread.
I like watching TV, it is clever and nice.
I like touching babies, they are really lazy.
I like seeing the rain, it drips on me.
I like listening to my teachers, they are nice.
I like the wind, it blows on me.
I like the sun, it shines on me.
I like the trees, they are green.
I like the stars, they twinkle on me.

Ruqiya Ahmed (8)
Hyndburn Park Primary School

Happiness

Happiness is having a sleepover at my grandma's
Happiness is watching a Liverpool match
Happiness is joining clubs
Happiness is eating sweets and chocolate
Happiness is a DS and a Game Boy
Happiness is birds singing
Happiness is helping my uncle in his workshop
Happiness is jumping up and down
Happiness is having a laugh.

Adam Hussain (8)
Hyndburn Park Primary School

Using My Senses

I like to sniff roses and they smell so nice
I like to eat curry but it makes my nose runny
I like hearing big popping balloons and then make one myself
I like looking at stars because they twinkle on me
I like the sun because it shines on me.

Zoiya Mahmood (8)
Hyndburn Park Primary School

Using My Senses

I like smelling rice, because it is very, very nice and it smells good
I like watching my plasma television and I always think
I'm going to have lots of vision
I like walking past the houses when I see loads of mice
I like touching soft blankets because they feel so good
I like seeing my pretty teachers always smiling
Because it's good seeing people smile
I like listening to tall and short teachers
Because they talk about important things and they talk a lot.

Saliha Maqsood (9)
Hyndburn Park Primary School

Using My Senses

I like hearing big popping balloons
But then they make my ears hurt.
I like to talk to people who listen,
I imagine them on a rough roller coaster.
I like watching 'Cheaper By The Dozen'
It's good to have a lot of people in your family.
I like walking to Paradise Park,
I see a farm on the way.

Junaid Ahmed (8)
Hyndburn Park Primary School

Happiness

Happiness is having a sleepover
Happiness is going on a holiday
Happiness is a nice cool glass of apple juice
Happiness is celebrating Eid with my family
Happiness is having a nature walk
Happiness is going to another city and seeing sights
Happiness is watching Coronation Street.

Barakah Shazad (8)
Hyndburn Park Primary School

Happiness

Happiness is when I go to the beach and I choose an ice lolly
Happiness is when I get birthday presents
Happiness is when I paint in school
Happiness is when I buy sweets
Happiness is when I go on my holidays
Happiness is when I get a burger meal deal
Happiness is when I get new clothes
Happiness is when I go to Pakistan.

Sidra Hussain (8)
Hyndburn Park Primary School

Happiness

Happiness is reading a new car book
Happiness is having a new art set
Happiness is buying new toy cars
Happiness is getting a new laptop
Happiness is eating ice cream
Happiness is drinking Coca-Cola
Happiness is going ice skating.

Sikandar Ali (8)
Hyndburn Park Primary School

Happiness

Happiness is riding my bike.
Happiness is playing football or cricket in the park.
Happiness is a game of tig.
Happiness is watching TV with my family.
Happiness is writing in class.
Happiness is colouring at school.
Happiness is playing conkers with my friends.

Anas Mahmood (8)
Hyndburn Park Primary School

Happiness

Happiness is sitting in my dad's BMW
Happiness is riding a mountain bike on a mountain
Happiness is imagining that you are eating lots of ice cream
Happiness is going shopping on my own and buying lots of junk
Happiness is going on a scary adventure
Happiness is being rich
Happiness is having fun.

Ayesha Hussain (8)
Hyndburn Park Primary School

On My Way To School

This morning, as I was on my way to school
The world outside started acting badly
The storm started rustling and whistling
The birds singing in the storm
Tornado spinning round and round
Then the cars started jumping, running, running
Bus doors sneezing open and shut
Cars coughing and spluttering, trying to push in
Lorries belching smoke, wheezing brakes
Dustbins rolling down the road angrily
Car lights blinking all the time
Dogs running around the place
The blue sky blowing in the wind
Aeroplanes screaming in mid-air
Fences standing straight as soldiers
Leaves covered the ground like a lady's hair
Pick-up truck honking as if shouting
Trees waving their branches
Bikes straining with weight of a rider
Old cigarettes lying on the floor
Helicopter chopping the air
On my way to school.

Natalie Fairhurst (10)
Millbrook CP School

The Workman Of Wood

He awoke in his rocking chair as he does so every morn
With a half-empty beer he stroked the head of his beloved pet deer
He walked over to the window to look down the valley of Aztec
And saw his precious wild pet.

Many a masterpiece had he made
To the people he sold, he hardly ever got paid
Once he picked up his tool
He didn't feel like a fool
Thus he was the Workman of Wood.

The Workman cut the wood asunder
And made a bed with a man deep in slumber
He cleanly smoothed the work piece
And moved it to the window
Thus he was the Workman of Wood.

Overlooking his work was as hard as pie
3.14159
For every mistake he made
He definitely didn't get paid
Thus he was the Workman of Wood.

When his day was over and done with
He celebrated with a visit
To the parlour for a beer
Went back to his chair
To wake in the morn
Thus he was the Workman of Wood.

Ben Foster (10)
Millbrook CP School

Well Done Wigan! You Rule!

W igan are the best
E xcitement builds
L oving every second
L eaving the coach in despair

D azzling fireworks
O h my goodness, the crowd is wild
N ever boo the opponents
E nd of a match is a way off

W ill you pass to me?
I s that a goal or what?
G ame is ace
A re we cool? Yes
N asty opponents are tackling me

Y ikes, don't hurt me
O h my, time flies by
U lcers are being bitten, ouch!

R otten smell of sweat
U nder the brave faces are scared brains
L eave me here why don't you
E y, I'm only nine years old!

Charlie Bennett (9)
Millbrook CP School

Football

F antastic
O ffside
O h no
T ime up
B all
A mazing
L oud
L ively.

Louis Ward (8)
Millbrook CP School

The Bad Trip To School

This morning as I was on my way to school
The world outside started behaving badly
The cars honked their horns
As if they were shouting at each other.

The buses revved their engines at the lollipop lady
As if they were growling at her
In return, the lollipop stick beamed at them
As if it was smirking.

I walked past an alleyway
Where the dustbins
Who were overflowing
Seemed like they were throwing bin bags back up.

I came to a bus stop
Children were lined up outside
The bus was coughing and spluttering
As though it was ill.

Finally, I came to the school
And looked at the building
I saw the children playing
And I was glad my journey was over.

Alexander Burns & Matthew McFadden (10)
Millbrook CP School

Happiness Is . . .

Happiness is playing football with my little brother
Happiness is drawing with my brother
Happiness is listening to JLS singing 'Everybody In Love'
Happiness is playing Lego Star Wars
Happiness is playing and watching Wonder Pets with my little brother
Happiness is having a laugh with my mates
Happiness is keeping my room a mess
Happiness is drawing dinosaurs.

Matthew Stockley (7)
Millbrook CP School

Chunky The Monkey

There once was a little monkey
And people called him Chunky
He liked to swing from tree to tree
But then the tree he did not see

It hit his face with such a bang
He just so yelled twee and wang
The day he found Bob and Fred
They were still and lying dead

Bob and Fred were lying dead
It could have been what they said
Or the monster that was not fed

Bob was good
And liked mud
Fred was bad
But mostly sad

So come on down
To Bridgfield Town
And you'll meet Chunky
The adventurous monkey.

Owen Vizard (10)
Millbrook CP School

River Severn

Splashing stream
Bog maker
Steep shimmerer
Fast meanders
Tall mountains
Wide meadows
Flat fields
High hills
Flood plains.

Andrew Cheetham (10)
Millbrook CP School

A Bad School Day

This morning as I was going to school
The world around me started to behave badly
The wind was whistling very loudly
And the dustbin was rolling down the hill madly
The helicopter chopped through the sky
When my imaginary friend said, 'Oh my.'
The car headlights blinked quite fast
As I got to the bottom of the hill I said, 'At last.'
'Still a long way to go!' said the trees dancing
I sat back in my chair
When the chair behind me started prancing
Lorries belching smoke, not a very good sight
As I approached the end of the tunnel
I had an accident in fright
It was buses sneezing doors open
As I inserted my bus token
Finally I got there
What a pain
Two minutes to go
I'm never going that way again!

Elliot Innocent (10)
Millbrook CP School

One, Two, Three

One, two, the cow goes moo
Three, four, I'm on a tour
Five, six, let's get a brick
Seven, eight, clean your plate
Nine, ten, where's a hen?
Eleven, twelve, thirteen, fourteen
I'm not a teen
Fifteen, sixteen, seventeen, eighteen
Nineteen, twenty
I need plenty.

Alex Morgan (9)
Millbrook CP School

River

Big river
Small fish
Flowing with the wind
With falling rocks
Crackly sound
Flying spray
Big meanders
Hot air
Large rocks
Crashing everywhere
Large waves
Interesting sights
Blue as the sea
Clean as clean
Tiny waves
Deep as deep
Big heaps.

Brandon Talbot (11)
Millbrook CP School

A Driving Car

Turn left, turn right
It drives all night
Turn left, turn right
Its wheels turn all night.
Turn left, turn right
It is very bright
Turn left, turn right
I have some light
And it shines all night.
Turn left, turn right
I'm going to the station
Turn left, turn right
And the answer is a *car!*

Amy Olivia-Sharkey (8)
Millbrook CP School

Bad Day

This morning I was on my way to school
The world outside me started behaving badly
The vicious wind knocked the angry bins over
The poor cans inside got dizzy and nervous.

The cars would honk their horns
As if to say, 'Get out of my way!'
The trucks' exhausts would splat and splutter
And their headlights would blink
The happy sky would look over the almighty world
The birds would then start to chatter
And also the wind would whistle.

The rain would show off and seek attention
And the lollipop sign would say he was better
The trees would dance in the wind
The sun would shine and the planes would fly angrily
All on my way to school!

Matthew Turner (10)
Millbrook CP School

Cats And Hair

Cats and hair, that's all I ever say,
Every day and night,
Whilst eating my tea
Watching TV
Even in bed
Everywhere I go
To my friends and family
This is what I say
Cats and hair
Every day
Cats and hair!

Faye Gillan (8)
Millbrook CP School

Lakes And Mountains

Lakes on end
Mountains all around
Bogs on the mountains
Streams all around
Fish jumping up
Fish going down
What a sensation
To our world.

Surfers on the foam
Mud falling down
Everyone on boats
Fishing all around
The sun is shining
Days on end
Clouds with frowns
And rain with pain.

Andy Matfen (10)
Millbrook CP School

Golf Tour

1, 2, 3, 4, where is the golf tour?
5, 6, 7, 8, that's great mate
9, 10, 11, 12, why is there an elf on the pitch?
12, 14, 15, 16, why's Hirstun here? He's rubbish
17, 18, 19, 20, want some food? No, got plenty
21, 22, 23, 24, this really is a golf tour
25, 26, 27, 28, wow, that was a good shot
Aye, it was, it was great.

29, 30, 31, 32, do you know where the loo is?
33, 34, 35, 36, didn't know there was Weetabix
37, 38, 39, 40, that is very naughty
41, 42, 43, 44, so where is the next golf tour?
45, 46, 47, 48, don't tell me, you're going to skate.

Joe Lowe (8)
Millbrook CP School

The Red Dust

People walking here and there
Minding their own business
Then a violent windstorm comes
Crashing like lightning
Mighty dust as red as the sun
Blazing through the skies
People wondering what is happening
Shutting all their doors
But no one knows why the red dust is floating, floating, floating.

See them peep
Through dusty windows
As the dust passes through
Sending cries from every corner
Looking up at the shocking view
The windstorm coming is such a shock
But no one knows why the red dust is blowing, blowing, blowing.

Georgia Woodcock (10)
Millbrook CP School

Grandma's House

G randma lets me watch telly late
R ound Grandma's garden is fun
A mazing frogs and toads
N ice food, she makes delicious food
D ance music, she has loads
M agnificent things to do
A mazing it is there, you would love it
'S he's a lovely grandma

H allowe'en parties we have loads
O h, her house is spooky at Hallowe'en
U sually loads of time we have to sleep
S o she is a lovely grandma
E xciting it is.

Max Cochrane (7)
Millbrook CP School

42

River

Artist lover
Flowing down the valley
Fast flowing destructor
Ripple

River
A slow, soft meander
Always shining under sunlight
And *splash!*

River
Estuary
Ending of the river
Ever helping to fill the sea
Gurgle.

Marcus Grimshaw (11)
Millbrook CP School

Henry Tudor

H ad six wives
E xecuted two
N ightmare as Jane died
R eally cruel to Anne
Y ou're beheaded

T udors
U tterly gross
D ie for a crime
O n the block
R eady to see blood spill?

Tom Moat (9)
Millbrook CP School

Astley Hall

A stley Hall
S uch a scary place
T ry to get in
L isten to the noise
E xecuted, executed
Y ou're dead

H ey, do you want to get in?
A ll you need to do is knock on the door
L isten to the noise
L isten to the noise.

Alex Cunliffe (9)
Millbrook CP School

Zack

Z ack
A ctive little puppy
C ute and cuddly
K ind and caring

My puppy Zack
He takes me on walks and nearly talks
To tell me that he loves me
I play hide-and-seek with him
Nobody can take him away from me
My puppy Zack!

Danielle Armstrong (9)
Millbrook CP School

The Moon And The Stars

The moon and the stars shine so bright,
Especially at night
The stars are glorious
The stars are cheery
Just like you.

The stars are happy, the moon is glorious
Just like you
The moon is glorious especially when it smiles
The moon is cheery too
The moon and the stars are friends too.

Stephanie Hart (9)
Millbrook CP School

Playground

P lay
L unchtime
A pple bobbing
Y oghurt
G round
R ace
O ffside
U niversal
N o nastiness
D eserted.

Jack Baron (7)
Millbrook CP School

Millbrook

M any people having fun
I nteresting lessons
L aughter in the playground
L ovely people
B eautiful loving school
R ain doesn't stop the fun
O utstanding
O utside is fun
K ind school.

Erin Chard (7)
Millbrook CP School

Happiness Is . . .

Playing with my mum
Doing sports
Dancing with my cousin Fran
Going to school
Playing on the computer
Playing in my bedroom
Playing school in my room
Watching Hannah Montana
Doing golden time.

Jessica Eastham (7)
Millbrook CP School

Family

F unny
A mazing
M um and Maddy
I ncredible
L ucy
Y ummy.

Jessica Kate Wilcock (7)
Millbrook CP School

Butterfly Fields

The beautiful sky is duck-egg blue
Where the sun is shining, that is true
The clouds are as soft as can be
If you will just come with me
Be free to fly with the butterflies
Just you and I
And don't wear your tie
Just come and fly with the butterflies.

Madeleine Wilcock (9)
Millbrook CP School

Presents

P resents
R eally wrapped
E normous
S pecial
E xcited
N ervous
T oy
S mall.

Oliver Green (7)
Millbrook CP School

Happiness

Happiness is golden time at school
Happiness is when my Pokémon evolve on my DS
Happiness is being with my family
Happiness is playing with my sisters
Happiness is getting smiles
Happiness is being with my friends
Happiness is great
Happiness is me and Isobel.

Joshua White (7)
Millbrook CP School

Skeleton

S cary bones
K nees knocking
E lbows crack
L ong legs and long arms
E very step
T urns me around
O h
N o!

Gina Caldwell (9)
Millbrook CP School

Happiness Is Everything

Happiness is watching TV
Happiness is playing golf with my friends
Happiness is listening to my dad playing also singing
Happiness is playing with people
Happiness is making people laugh and have fun
Happiness is making people annoyed like my sister
Happiness is to play on the playground with people
Happiness is golden time.

Sarah Elsden (8)
Millbrook CP School

Happiness Is . . .

Happiness is playing with my cats
Happiness is training my cats
Happiness is playing with my friends
Happiness is doing numbers at school
Happiness is watching TV
Happiness is building snowmen
Happiness is going home.

Isobel Lowe (7)
Millbrook CP School

Dancing

D ancing
A mazing
N ice music
C ool
 I ncredible
N ice dresses
G roovy.

Chloe Hare (7)
Millbrook CP School

Happiness Is . . .

Happiness is candy
Happiness is sweets
Happiness is peaceful
Happiness is fab
Happiness is hilarious
Happiness is lovable
Happiness is jolly.

Bethany Wilkins (7)
Millbrook CP School

Spider

S ilky spider sitting on a web
P ulling a log for a home
 I t is running in circles like mad
D ancing in the dangerous mud puddles
E ating on the mud and on the litter
R unning in all the wet and soggy, sinking mud.

Jamie Ward (7)
Millbrook CP School

Tudors

T udors
U tterly gross
D oors are creaking
O pening slowly
R oaring Henry the VIII
S earching the house for priests.

Elliot Baughan (9)
Millbrook CP School

Happiness Is . . .

Happiness is listening to music
Happiness is playing with my friends
Happiness is piggybacks
Happiness is sleepovers at my friend's
Happiness is watching TV
Happiness is watching rugby.

Elisha Cahir (7)
Millbrook CP School

Sports

S wimmers
P ool
O utside
R unners
T ennis
S winging.

Abigail Ainscough (7)
Millbrook CP School

Happiness Is . . .

Happiness is playing games
Happiness is watching TV
Happiness is playing
Happiness is sitting next to my friend
Happiness is going to Millbrook.

Daniel Jenkins (7)
Millbrook CP School

Snake

S lithering through the grass
N ear to the people
A long tail
K eeps swaying
E ach person screams, *'Snake!'*

Rebecca Kay (8)
Millbrook CP School

Happiness Is . . .

Happiness is listening to my favourite music, JLS
Happiness is me and my friends playing our favourite game
Happiness is at Hallowe'en going trick or treating with my friends
Happiness is going on holiday to America.

Ellie Addison (7)
Millbrook CP School

Little Frog - Haiku

Little frog stopping
Bouncing on the lily pads
Little frog stop now.

Olivia O'Brien (9)
Queen's Drive Primary School

Untitled

Roses are red
Violets are blue
I love flowers
Which are blue.

Roses are red
Violets are blue
I love plants
Especially trees.

Roses are red
Violets are blue
I love nature
Especially here.

Roses are red
Violets are blue
I enjoyed my poem
Hope you did too.

Samson Giranta Mwita (11)
Queen's Drive Primary School

It's Nearly Christmas!

It's nearly October half-term
So I know it's nearly Christmas
Hallowe'en and Bonfire Night
So I know it's nearly Christmas
The nights are drawing in
And it's dark when I get home
Mist and fog are all about
And it's tremendously cold
'I can't wait for Christmas,' I shout to my mum
Before dreaming of all the great times we'll have
Which will be so much fun
And that's because it's nearly Christmas!

Thomas Grundy (10)
Queen's Drive Primary School

Haunted House

As I entered the gate, shiver went my bones
The wind all blowing in different tones
I opened the door with such a creak
It felt as if it took a week
As soon as I stepped inside
I felt petrified
I heard a high-pitched scream
It felt as if I was being struck by a laser beam
The cobwebs all around me
I heard a strange noise like a bee
As I went to discover the sound
It was obvious I was bound
To run away screaming.

Ella Aldridge (9)
Queen's Drive Primary School

The Misty Forest

He stepped into the forest where the dragon lurked
He would surely die, what a jerk
With no common sense he went further
No one would've gone away from his mother.

What a dumbo, what a saddo
I would be very glad though
Because I didn't really like him
He was easy to eat because he was slim.

So don't go into the misty forest
You'll just get eaten like the rest
In case you haven't realised, I'm the dragon
So don't charge at me with a wagon!

Isaac Ellis (10)
Queen's Drive Primary School

Let's Party With The Girls And Boys

I've got my jeans on and I'm running around
We're gonna go to the dance in the middle of the ground
Everybody's getting up in their PJs
We're gonna go to the disco in the middle of the ground.

I've got my same skirt on and I'm walking around
We're gonna go to the disco in the middle of the town
Everybody's getting up in their nighties
We're gonna go to the disco in the middle of the town.

Lucy Grant (10)
Queen's Drive Primary School

Animals

A ntarctic penguins stroll around
N oisy crickets click very loudly
I nsects walk ever so fast
M any more I can tell
A round and around the atmosphere
L eopards leap ever so high
S o why don't I get a butterfly?

Ruth Buckley (9)
Queen's Drive Primary School

My Brother

My brother is very naughty and he looks so warty
My brother is smelly, he also loves strawberry jelly
My brother is not so clever, but he likes to predict the weather
My brother loves money, so he'll buy a shop of honey
My brother is short and likes to play sport
These are the properties of my brother
So don't make me have another!

Humza Rafique (10)
Queen's Drive Primary School

Lightning

Lightning, lightning
Is so frightening
Lightning, lightning
Is so terrifying
Lightning, lightning in the sky
I think it's after my school tie.

Sabrina Sadiq (9)
Queen's Drive Primary School

Snowflakes

Snowflakes everywhere, icicles here and there
Snowflakes floating about in the pink and white air
People with gloves and people with hats
Playing in the snow tracks
It must be cold, it must be white
It's always on my right-hand side.

Parvinder Kaur (9)
Queen's Drive Primary School

Tiger

T ramping everywhere
I am leaping here and there
G rowling here and there so beware
E choing everywhere, so you will see me here and there
R oaring fiercely, so you will hear me clearly.

Zak Johnson (9)
Queen's Drive Primary School

Bunny

There was once a little bunny
That was so very funny
She made others laugh
By riding on a giraffe
So now she has lots of money.

Zohia Shabbir (9)
Queen's Drive Primary School

Abbie

A bbie is best
B etter than the rest
B e like me, I am the best
I can eat you so beware
E at you up for dinner!

Abbie Whitehouse (9)
Queen's Drive Primary School

Happiness

Happiness is the colour yellow, like the bright sun
Beating down on the happy families at the park
Happiness looks like the joy on a child's face
Whilst opening their presents
Happiness smells like the fresh sweet strawberries growing in a
                                        farmer's field
Happiness sounds like little children laughing out loud
Whilst watching their favourite TV show
Happiness feels like you're in a magical world
With the emerald waterfalls surrounding you
Whilst listening to the water gushing into the gentle lakes
Happiness reminds me of the happy children playing in the park.

Zamira Brown (9)
St Anne's CE Primary School, Wigan

Fun

Fun is multicoloured like a huge swirl of fun ideas
Things to do for the day ahead
Fun smells like sweet lollipops
Hanging in the prettily decorated sweet shop on a warm sunny day
Fun looks like a happy family zooming down the log flume tracks at
Camelot
Then getting drenched to the bone by freezing cold water at the
bottom

Fun feels like the shivering feeling
That runs down the back of your bony spine
When a cold breeze hits you then suddenly passes by
Fun sounds like a group of babies giggling away together
At the red-nosed clown standing on the stage
Pulling out a cute rabbit from his magic cage
Fun reminds me of when I was little
And my mum, my dad, my sister and I
All went on a day out to the park
And me and my sister played in the golden sandpit
Whilst my mum and my dad joyfully watched us.

Charlotte Farnworth (11)
St Anne's CE Primary School, Wigan

Fun

Fun is the colour of the warm, shiny sunshine
Gleaming on the faces of the children playing in the park
Fun looks like adults romantically having a picnic down at the
seaside
Whilst their children are playing in the sea
Fun smells like a slice of chocolate cake
Inflated with chocolate chips and drizzled with chocolate sauce
Fun sounds like children's laughter shouting out to the world
Fun feels like the sun beating down on your face as you play
Fun reminds me of when I was little
And I laughed for the first time.

Kelsey Jade Tither (9)
St Anne's CE Primary School, Wigan

Emotions Rhyme

When you know that sadness is around
You will surely shrink to the ground
When you know that fun is around
You will most likely astound

When you feel loneliness is here
You will find friends at Wigan Pier
When you feel anger is here
Run away and do not fear

When you see that love is there
You just run and tell the mayor
When you see that silence is there
There will be nothing but you and a hair.

This is the end of my emotions rhyme
Hope you will listen again next time.

Kieran Molloy (10)
St Anne's CE Primary School, Wigan

Sadness

Sadness is blue like a tear running down your blotchy face
Sadness is red when anger takes its place
Sadness looks like a waterfall dribbling into a lake
Sadness is like a bad day when you're not awake
Sadness sounds like an animal moaning to be fed
Sadness sounds like a woman crying when suddenly being divorced
after being wed
Sadness feels like a war that goes on and on and on
Sadness feels like an illness that's never gone
Sadness reminds me of the dead and departed
Sadness reminds me of the people that are cold-hearted.

Alarna Greenheart (11)
St Anne's CE Primary School, Wigan

Excitement

Excitement is pink like a child's pink cheeks
After playing outside in the garden
Excitement looks like a woman dancing
At the ball she's always wished for
Excitement smells like a teenager opening her box of perfume
On her birthday and spraying it on her wrist
Excitement sounds like two birds tweeting
On an old oak tree branch
Excitement feels like a new father
Holding his baby girl and rocking her to sleep
Excitement reminds me of the first time I started to ride my bike.

Lydia Challinor (9)
St Anne's CE Primary School, Wigan

Excitement

Excitement is multicoloured
Like children playing in a pit full of balls
Excitement looks like children opening Christmas presents on Jesus'
birthday
Excitement smells like a roast dinner
With potatoes and a roast chicken soaked in a bed of gravy
Excitement sounds like two children on a see-saw bouncing up and
down
Excitement feels like a volcano inside of me that's ready to explode
Excitement reminds me of opening my birthday presents.

James Crank (9)
St Anne's CE Primary School, Wigan

Love

Love is gold like the shimmering stars in the moonlit sky
Love looks like a flickering fire, warm and cosy in the fireplace
Love smells like a fully blossomed rose
That a friend gives you on Valentine's Day
Love sounds like doves tweeting to one another that makes you
                                                    sleepy
Love feels like a cake smothered in melted chocolate
With two scoops of chocolate ice cream melting in your mouth
Love reminds me of looking up at the stars on a golden sandy beach
Thinking of what the future holds for me.

Alex Freeman (10)
St Anne's CE Primary School, Wigan

Love

Love is red like a love heart filled with hugs
Love looks like a bunch of roses that your friend has given you
Love smells like a bed of petals waiting for me to fall on and go to
                                                    sleep
Love sounds like a little girl giving her mum a kiss
And telling her she loves her
Love feels like you're lying on a couch watching a film
With a blanket over you to keep you nice and warm
Love reminds me of when I used to hug my dad at night.

Kerri Lowe (9)
St Anne's CE Primary School, Wigan

Fun

F un is like little children whooshing down a water slide screaming
U nlimited toys to play with are fun for every child
N ever bored when fun is around
   the laughter and joy is a wonderful sound.

Jessica Roughley (10)
St Anne's CE Primary School, Wigan

Sadness

Sadness is the colour of a light blue teardrop
Rolling down the soft cheek of a baby's face
Sadness looks like your mother and father going through a divorce
And walking out the door
Sadness smells like rotten food your mother never put in the bin
Sadness sounds like your mother crying in pain because your father
left
Sadness is like a heart breaking inside a crying body
Sadness reminds me of your mother and father arguing.

Georgia Bridge (10)
St Anne's CE Primary School, Wigan

Fun

Fun is lots of different colours like a rainbow in the baby-blue sky
Fun looks like a ginormous fudge cake with lots of multicoloured
Smarties and a dollop of ice cream with strawberry sauce
Fun smells like a soft breeze in the air
Fun sounds like lots of little children laughing in the park
Whilst swinging high on the swings
Fun feels like the cold water spraying out of your friend's water gun
On a bright sunny day.

Hannah Tempest (9)
St Anne's CE Primary School, Wigan

Fun

Fun is the colour of orange because it is not dark and not light
Fun looks like children playing on a roller coaster
Fun smells like a chocolate ice cream being eaten in a cake
Fun sounds like children laughing on the swings
Fun feels like touching your McDonald's chicken burger
Fun reminds me of my parties at all the different places.

Cameron Bennett (9)
St Anne's CE Primary School, Wigan

Stress

The colour of stress is red fading into black
Stress looks like someone scissor-kicking you in the face
Stress smells like a burning hot dog
Stress sounds like someone screaming and shouting
And your brain throbbing like it's going to explode
Stress feels like being tied to a pole and struggling to get off
Stress reminds me of being bullied
And footballs being kicked at you.

Sam Boyd (10)
St Anne's CE Primary School, Wigan

Loneliness

Loneliness is like a black cloud covering the bright yellow sun
It never moves, like rain in a storm
Loneliness feels like a heartbreak every day
It feels like a cut never getting better
Feeling afraid to trust anyone
Afraid to make new friends
Loneliness is the colour of bark on a tree
Dark and gloomy or like the never-ending whiteness on a misty day.

Paige Banks (10)
St Anne's CE Primary School, Wigan

Happiness

Happiness is blue like the light blue sky
With white clouds in it passing by
Happiness looks like children playing in the sand
And having lots of fun
Happiness smells like the very air we breathe
And children laughing with joy
Happiness sounds like playing out with my mates
Happiness reminds me of when I used to play with my hamster.

Josh Parker Pugh (10)
St Anne's CE Primary School, Wigan

Crazy Shopping

I went to a shop and this is what I got
A dinosaur egg
A hippo's leg
And a bird's beak that looked like a peg.

I went to a shop and this is what I got
An evil-looking creature
The smallest teacher
And St Anne's radio's special feature.

I went to a shop and this is what I got
Some boring old lead
A monster hiding under a bed
Oh wait, maybe a microwave instead.

I went to a shop and this is what I got
A bumbling bee
A whooshing sea
And a person that looked exactly like me.

I went to a shop and this is what I got
A person called Sue
A cow that went moo
And a bird that shouted, 'Cuckoo, cuckoo.'

I bought all the place
Nothing left, not even a shoelace
Just full of empty space.

I stopped going to the store
Because it was a bore
There was nothing in
Not even a tin
But the shopkeeper still had a grin!

Abigail Garratty (11)
St Anne's RC Primary School, Blackburn

Friends

Friends are loving
Friends are kind
Friends won't kick
Your beautiful behind.

Friends are patient
Do some bone work
Friends will help you
Do your homework.

Friends are nice
Friends are gentle
If you annoy them
They'll go mental.

Friends are the best
Friends don't fight
Friends will guide you
Through the night.

Friends are cool
Friends are caring
Friends will give
'Cause you are sharing.

Getting on together
Should be forever.

Ibrahim Patel (10)
St Anne's RC Primary School, Blackburn

My Cat Garfield

My cat Garfield is as orange as marmalade
He is as fast as an elephant
His whiskers are as bright as the moonlight
His eyes are as black as a bat
His claws are as sharp as a shark's tooth.

Shannon Horrocks
St Anne's RC Primary School, Blackburn

My Magic Lunch Box
(Based on 'Magic Box' by Kit Wright)

I will put in my magic lunch box . . .
The yummy taste of my favourite school dinner
A pizza straight from the oven
And the first time I ever ate duck pancakes.

I will put in my magic lunch box . . .
The sprinkles from a magical doughnut called Bob
The royal ketchup from the ketchup king
And a chocolate chip cookie dough monster.

I will put in my magic lunch box . . .
The smell of salt and vinegar chops covered in onion gravy
The sound of hot buttery popcorn in the microwave
And the taste of Brussels sprouts, yuck.

The recipe for my box is cookie dough
And chocolate chips and a fried egg for the lid
In the corners there are secret recipes
And the hinges of my box are strips of bacon.

I shall go to Candy Land in my lunch box
Then I'll go to the beach and swim in the chocolate sea
Then end up on a rainbow dust beach.

Ethan Yates (11)
St Anne's RC Primary School, Blackburn

A Dolphin

A dolphin is as pretty as the sky
His skin is as soft as a feather
His personality is as beautiful as the sea
His eyes twinkle like a star
His mouth is such a squeaky little thing
His tail is as pretty as a cloud
He jumps as high as a house
The best thing is that he was made by God.

Órla Rose McManamon
St Anne's RC Primary School, Blackburn

The Magic Box
(Based on 'Magic Box' by Kit Wright)

I will put in my box . . .
The smell of a baby's nappy bags
The first time I rode my bike
And a dolphin swimming in the deep blue sea.

I will put in my box . . .
The first time I went on holiday
The first raindrop of spring
And the bluest water from a lake.

I will put in my box . . .
The first time I hugged my parents
And a baby's first word.

My box is fashioned from bronze, silver and gold
With spikes on the lid and carrot sticks in the corners
Its hinges are as soft as a cushion.

I shall go to space in my box
To see a monkey doing the moon walk
Then go back to Earth in the lovely yellow sun.

Charli Hosker (10)
St Anne's RC Primary School, Blackburn

The Monster

As brown as mud
As fast as a cheetah
As loud as a lion
His eyes as red as blood
His ears are floppy like jelly
He is as wrinkly as my granny
As crazy as a chimpanzee
As tall as Blackburn College
Can you guess who it is?

Joseph Forkin (8)
St Anne's RC Primary School, Blackburn

The Magic Box
(Based on 'Magic Box' by Kit Wright)

I will put in my box . . .
A camel with three humps
Michael Jackson living till his 51st birthday
A monkey doing the moonwalk on the moon.

I will put in my box . . .
A monkey doing the robot
A two-legged lion with a pig's tail
A dizzy monkey dancing and singing his heart out.

I will put in my box . . .
A mommy with a Pierrot clown
A spineless snake with poison in its eyes
A horse charging down a bumpy old road.

My box is fashioned from a wizard's power
It is icy cold and encrusted with gold
The lid is covered in silver.

I will go in my box to Japan
And eat my lunch in a water garden.

Joshua Harris (10)
St Anne's RC Primary School, Blackburn

Delta Vienna

On 27th October my sister was born
With big bright eyes and silky skin
She took my breath away.

Delta Vienna is her name
Oh my gosh, I hope she's not a pain
But I'll still love her all the same.

Demie Martindale (10)
St Anne's RC Primary School, Blackburn

The Magic Box
(Based on 'Magic Box' by Kit Wright)

I will put in the box . . .
The sharpest claw of a crab
The longest tentacle of an octopus
The fastest crawl of a millipede.

I will put in the box . . .
The hairy leg of a spider
The high-pitched twitter of a bird
The scary roar of a lion.

I will put in the box . . .
The joke of a clownfish
The bloodthirsty jaw of a shark
The sharp sting of a bee.

My box is fashioned with the scales of a rainbow fish
With cats' eyes on the lid
And sharks' teeth in the corners.

Chloe Glover (10)
St Anne's RC Primary School, Blackburn

A Friend Is Like A Flower

A friend is like a flower
A rose to be exact
Or maybe like a brand new gate
That never comes unlatched
A friend is like an owl
Both beautiful and wise
Or perhaps a friend is like a ghost
Whose spirit never dies
A friend is like a heart that beats
Strong until the end
Where would we be in this world
If we didn't have a friend?

Halima Karbhari (10)
St Anne's RC Primary School, Blackburn

68

The Magnificent Box
(Based on 'Magic Box' by Kit Wright)

I will put in the box . . .
The sound of a baby laughing
The smell of the sea swishing and swirling
A picture of my grandad fishing with a smile on his face.

I will put in the box . . .
The first kiss of a boy
A blue diamond from under the ground
A Spanish dancer spinning around in the light of the moon.

My box is fashioned from the reddest ruby
With stars in the corners
Its hinges are made out of hope.

I shall change time which once went bad
And I will change it to good
I will go to Australia and look after the animals
And go to France to see the stars.

Jessica Gaul (10)
St Anne's RC Primary School, Blackburn

This Is The Right Thing For Me

Cheetahs pouncing, lions roaring
Toast in the morning
That's just right for me
Butter on potatoes, potatoes in a bowl
Yum, that's just right for me
Sugar on my breakfast
Sugar on my peas
Do you want a bit of mine?
Taste of strawberries
Taste of blueberries
Taste of blackberries
Please don't tell me, I am in Heaven.

Beth Harvey (9)
St Bernadette's RC Primary School, Lancaster

Everything I Like

I like music to my ears
And it goes, *bang, bang*
And it really hurts, but I don't care.

My favourite taste is chocolate
Chocolate is my favourite food
Melts in your mouth till it's all gone
Yummy, yummy in my tummy
It is chocalicious
Bite, bite and yum-yum, scrummy

I like to feel my brother's back
Warm and soft, cuddly, very cute

I see
Roses in Grandma's garden
Pink, white, red
Red as red wine
I feel happy whenever I see them
It's nice when they're blooming.

Niamh Cooney-Millar (8)
St Bernadette's RC Primary School, Lancaster

Chelsea T-Shirts And Joe

I like to see Chelsea T-shirts
I don't like the new one
It looks like a rugby T-shirt
But I love the old one
With their sponsor Samsung.

I like to see Joe
He helps me in everything
And I do too
If he's sad
I make him happy
And the same to me.

Ahmad Mahmoud (8)
St Bernadette's RC Primary School, Lancaster

70

I Love Doughnuts

I love doughnuts, yes I do
Jammy, yummy too
Like a falling asteroid
In the middle of the sky.
Why don't you give it a try
I love doughnuts, yes I do
In chocolate sprinkles
Icing and sugar too
I like giving them to my mother
I love doughnuts, yes I do
They smell like Heaven
With angels too.

Henry Moorby (8)
St Bernadette's RC Primary School, Lancaster

My World Of Sense

I love to see the sun so bright
Shining through the bushes of trees
My favourite taste, spaghetti in the morning
The tingling sensation of the tomato sauce
The softness of the cotton
From a sheep so warm
And comfy like a cover
I can smell the fruit from the market stall
So pretty and nice
I like to hear the trees blowing
Like whooshing music in the night.

Miri Kim (8)
St Bernadette's RC Primary School, Lancaster

What I Like Best

I love to see a view of a beach
With the hot sun around me
I like the feel of lovely silk
It fells nice and fuzzy
My favourite taste is strawberry milk
It's very sweet as it runs down my throat
It feels so cold in autumn days
When it's very windy
I love to see trees blow
I love the colour of autumn leaves
That's what I love the best.

Hannah Short (8)
St Bernadette's RC Primary School, Lancaster

My Favourite Things

Puppies' and kittens' fur is so soft, so is rabbits'
I like animals, but that's not all
Chocolate, sweets, cream too
They are more of my favourite things
Music, birds singing, dogs barking
That is what I like to hear
And the smell of flowers and perfume
Makes the air smell better
I like to taste chocolate and sweets
Cream as well
But to make it taste better I add sugar.

Ellie Auty (9)
St Bernadette's RC Primary School, Lancaster

Animals

White lions look like white kittens
Kittens wake up early to play a game
Kittens look like little white mice
Little white mice like to nibble on cheese
And also on your toes
White mice like white ants
Ants eat your waste
That you put in your garbage bin
They eat your fruit and eat your veg
And white animals are the best.

Evie Smith (8)
St Bernadette's RC Primary School, Lancaster

My Favourite Things

I like to see the morning colours of all the beautiful roses
They come in so many colours like pink and red and white
I like to smell the gingerbread men just come out of the oven
Then we put on the tasty icing, now it's time to eat
I like to hear the sound of cherry wood burning and crackling
It's a big delight
I like to taste strawberries and marshmallows
Especially covered in chocolate
If you really want me to then I would even sleep in them
These are a few of my favourite things.

Jessica Ireland (8)
St Bernadette's RC Primary School, Lancaster

I Like Peanut Butter

I like the taste of peanut butter because it is so thick
And it stays in your mouth
I love the taste of chocolate
Because it is really sweet and long-lasting
Rice Krispie cakes are really crunchy
Pancakes are really chewy
And you can spread anything on them
I like to feel silk dressing gowns
I like to feel marble tables, the smoothness is really nice.

Juliet Lavelle (8)
St Bernadette's RC Primary School, Lancaster

Dogs Are . . .

Dogs are cute, soft, adorable
I shouldn't forget cosy
Dogs bark, howl and growl.

They smell like a pink rose
Dogs feel like a pink petal, so soft
They run like a cheetah

Dogs are big softies
That's what I like!

Erin Poppy Barratt (8)
St Bernadette's RC Primary School, Lancaster

I Love

I love the sound of music
I love to have some cheese
I love the smell of petrol
I love the feel of silk
These are my favourite things
And I love them very much.

Josef Verbic (8)
St Bernadette's RC Primary School, Lancaster

74

The Things That I Do With My Senses

I like to wake and watch TV
My favourite programme is SpongeBob SquarePants on CITV.
I like to taste toast with a lot of chocolate on
With a bit of orange juice to lighten my day up
I love to hear my cats purring
They get a bit mad and then get off the sofa.

Mylene Bertrand (8)
St Bernadette's RC Primary School, Lancaster

I Like Chocolate

Chocolate is so brown like a chocolate cake
I think chocolate is delightful
And my favourite and it's the best for dessert
I like chocolate melted
It is as nice as custard
I love chocolate, it's the best.

Niamh McCrudden (8)
St Bernadette's RC Primary School, Lancaster

What I Like

I love to watch Preston football team
I love to hear all the crowd shout
I love the smell of freshly baked pies
I love the smell of aftershave
I like chips and lots of food
That's what I like.

Ciaran Sutcliffe (8)
St Bernadette's RC Primary School, Lancaster

The Toilet Of Doom!

The toilet of doom
Lives in the bathroom
When you need to go
'Ew, bad sight'
And he gives a great bite.

The toilet of doom
Lives in the bathroom
When you try to sit
It says, 'Sorry I bit.'

The toilet of doom
Lives in the bathroom
It behaves badly
Like my friend Bradley.

The toilet
The toilet of
The toilet of doom.

The toilet of doom
Lives in the bathroom
And has now *died!*

Rebecca Hartley (11)
St Mary's CE Primary School, Rochdale

Xmas

Not a mouse stirs
I saw a red light
In the night sky
Not a mouse stirs
I saw the bright moon
In the night sky
Not a mouse stirs
I saw my presents
In the bright early morning!

Paighton Ridgway (10)
St Mary's CE Primary School, Rochdale

Alarm Clock

'Get up, you lazy thing,' screeched my alarm clock
My alarm clock was screeching all morning.
'Shut up,' I yelled at my alarm clock
'You're so annoying!' I shouted at my alarm clock
My alarm clock screamed like a newborn baby
It was so loud.

My alarm clock pestered me until I opened my blue eyes.
'All right, all right, I'm up,' I shouted at my alarm clock
It still didn't shut up.

When I looked at my alarm clock
It was bouncing up and down
'Stop bouncing up and down,' I yelled
It was jumping up and down like a kangaroo
Finally the red little alarm clock stopped bouncing up and down like
a kangaroo

It was staring at me
The number three and number nine were glaring at me
It was very weird.

Charleigh Whiteman (10)
St Mary's CE Primary School, Rochdale

Untitled

I like the sea, the sea
Because it's blue
God made it for me and you
God made the animals, the animals for us
He gave us rain for the plants to grow
He made the trees for us
The trees for us
He made the sky for us
The sky for us
He made everything for us.

Rhys Thomond (7)
St Mary's CE Primary School, Rochdale

Inside A Boy's Head

Inside a boy's head (well mine)
I think about things all the time
I think about girls with diamonds and pearls
And dogs with little bow ties

Inside a boy's head (well mine)
I think about things all the time
I think about food, McDonald's, oh yeah dude
Inside a boy's head (well mine).

Inside a boy's head (well mine)
I think about things all the time
I think about my looks with my stylish hair cuts
I think about things all the time.

Inside a boy's head (well mine)
I think about things all the time
I think about school which is so uncool
Inside a boy's head . . . (well mine).

Ryan Karl Kershaw (10)
St Mary's CE Primary School, Rochdale

Night-Time Nasties

I was laying in my bed awake
When I saw something coming to my bed
But I knew it was only in my head
I heard the sound of the clock ticking
Tick, tock, tick
Coming closer to my bed
But I knew it was only in my head
Something climbed on the pole
Outside my window
But I knew it was only in my head
All the birds were ready to bite
'Quickly, quickly, turn on the light!'

Amy Jenkins (7)
St Mary's CE Primary School, Rochdale

Dark Streets

I walked down the terrifying streets
It was really, really dark
There was nobody around in the terrifying street
The trees were moving
I fell down a hole
I met a mole
I climbed back up and started walking again
I saw a house
It was scary and terrifying
It had scary shadows
I saw another one under a car
It looked like a little scary beast
I carried on walking
I saw a head but I knew it was my imagination
I went back home running really fast
My heart was beating
Home at last!

Farah Hussain (7)
St Mary's CE Primary School, Rochdale

The Lonely Chair

Lurking in the study was a breathing chair
A bleeding chair
It was so cold and red
I dragged it
Like a robber would drag his sack
He looked sad, very sad
Just sat there
All alone in the corner of the study
He was so silent
Didn't even move
Just like a dead man would lie in his coffin
I felt sorry for that chair
Just wished he wasn't there.

Adam Mullaney(10)
St Mary's CE Primary School, Rochdale

The Dirty Toothbrush

I am an old, rotten toothbrush
I don't know why this boy wants to put me in his mouth
I used to be blue with a picture of a football
But now I am rusty and dirty.

As I sit in the bathroom the door opens
I think, *I hope he hasn't come to brush his teeth*
I am already dirty and horrible
Yes, he has picked me up
He has put me in his mouth
I am going to get more dirty.
'Oh no!'
I am ugly and horrible
I hope he does not use me again
'Please God, make sure he doesn't use me again.'

Lorna Leigh Matthews (10)
St Mary's CE Primary School, Rochdale

Bathroom

I was getting ready for bed, all was quiet
And all that day I had been eating sweets
So I had to brush my teeth
As I squeezed the paste on my brush
It screamed at me
'Oh no, look at her horrible teeth
And I have to put my head in that mouth.'
My brush is like a human, it eats and talks and walks.

Then I had to have a bath because I had been playing football
As I climbed into the bath, she screeched,
'Oh no, look at that face, so dirty.'
I washed my face so sparkly and clean
My face looked nice now
She said, 'Oh hooray.'

Chloe Rushton (10)
St Mary's CE Primary School, Rochdale

80

The Alarm Clock

Every day my alarm clock cries, 'Wake up!'
Until I do and if I'm not up within twenty seconds
He jumps on me and says, 'Hey you, no one likes you
And you're gonna be late for school.'

When I get up he still screams
And even if everybody on the street stamps on him
He'll still get up and say, 'Oi you lot, get off me
Or you're gonna pay.'

After a while everybody got sick of him
So they dumped him on the Bermuda Triangle
And he still found his way home.

After a few years the alarm clock became sick
And eventually died.

Jacob Vere (10)
St Mary's CE Primary School, Rochdale

My Alarm Clock

When I go into my room
My alarm clock screams like a baby
I shout, 'Save me, save me, save me!'

I scream and shout and yell,
'Wake up you stupid thing.'
But it must be in a deep, deep sleep.

My alarm clock shakes and nudges me
And pokes like an angry monster
'Stop, shut up, just, just *stop!*'

My alarm clock pesters me and bullies me
And annoys me and it always tries to seek my attention.
'I've had it with you!'

Jessica Hopkins (11)
St Mary's CE Primary School, Rochdale

Untitled

When I'm walking in the dark
I see trees swooping
Like a group of witches on brooms
Trying to find me
But I know it's only in my head
I rush home to get in my bed
But I hear my mum
Banging up the stairs
Is it a demon creature trying to get into my room?
I know it's only in my head
Really it is my mum seeing if I'm asleep yet
Then I can see our cat on the window sill
Is it a dog trying to break the window?

Katie Rushton (8)
St Mary's CE Primary School, Rochdale

The Leaf Falling Off A Tree

One day
A leaf
Was falling
Off a tree.

The tree was
Rock hard
It hurt
The poor little leaf.

And the tree
And the leaf
Lived
Happily ever after.

Rebecca Mills (8)
St Mary's CE Primary School, Rochdale

Walking Home

As I walked down the creepy, pitch-black street
I saw shadows under the blue, spooky car
I know that it was only the shadow of the car
The people going trick or treating
Totally freaked me out
But I knew that they were only masks
Then I saw big Eddy
I went to bed
Then ghosts haunted me
I shouted, 'Mum, Dad!'
But I was home alone . . .
'Quickly, quickly, turn on the light!'

Sheldon Atkinson (7)
St Mary's CE Primary School, Rochdale

Lunch Box

It's lunchtime at school, hip hip hooray
You can hear all the children laughing and shouting
My packed lunch is alive, oh no
When I reach into my lunch box it bites me
I yell and scream, 'Oh no!'
Each time it's lunch I get hungry
Because my packed lunch eats my dinner
My packed lunch yells, 'You ugly thing.'
No one understands my packed lunch is alive
My lunch box annoys me
And it wants attention all the time.

Bethany Thompson (10)
St Mary's CE Primary School, Rochdale

The Nightmare

I was sleeping in my bed
When I woke up in my head
At night I was on the street
I saw a cat and a stranger behind me
I was not scared, I was not brave
I was terrified
I wanted to go back in my bed
But . . . then I realised
I was lost!
'Quickly, quickly
Turn on the light.'

Isabelle Hollis (7)
St Mary's CE Primary School, Rochdale

Untitled

Every morning when I wake up
My alarm clock goes crazy
He says I'm very lazy.

It jumps on me, shouts at me
Yells at me and orders me
And I feel like throwing it out of the window
But if I did throw it out of the window
It would never get me up for school.

Connor Williams (11)
St Mary's CE Primary School, Rochdale

The Cloud Watching Us

The rain is like a crying child
On a cloud in the sky
Sad and thoughtful
The man was always watching by

The rain is as sad as the man in the sky
When everyone is trying to watch by
The rain likes the sea just like a child loves water
And some people like rain too.

Ryu Dutton (10)
St Mary's CE Primary School, Rochdale

Down The Dark Path

I walked down a narrow path
As I got further down the path
I started to hear noises down the path
And shadows down the path
Scary people following me
As I walked to my friend's house . . .

Alexandra Metcalfe (7)
St Mary's CE Primary School, Rochdale

The Highwayman
(Inspired by 'The Highwayman' by Alfred Noyes)

The wind was a torrent of darkness
The moon let out a misty glow
The road was a band of pale moonlight
And the sound of the highwayman riding, riding, riding
Up to the old inn door.

He'd a light blue hat on his forehead
He'd a green long coat with a tail on it
His boots were long and black
He rode with a jewelled shine . . .
His rapier held a twinkle under the dim sky.

Over the cobbles he dashed in the dark inn yard
He kicked on the door
The door opened and Bess the landlord's daughter was
Standing, plaiting a dark red love knot
In her dark black hair.

Behind the door Tim the Ostler listened
He loved the landlord's daughter
Tim had a gun in his hand
He shot the highwayman down
He went down
Bess was sad, but happy, her love had died.

Chloe Wall (9)
St Peter's CE Primary School, Rochdale

The Highwayman
(Inspired by 'The Highwayman' by Alfred Noyes)

The wind was like the sea
The road was like the moon
The field was a ribbon of moonlight
But the highwayman came riding, riding, riding
Up to the old inn door.

He'd a French cocked hat, a bushy, mushy beard
He'd a coat of leather and a light creamy skin
That fitted with a jewelled twinkle
His boots were on his thigh.

The dusty black sky was like the sea
But somebody called Lea
Came riding with a winkle, winkle, winkle
Over the cobbles, clashed and banged
'Wow, I say, 'Bess is here.'
Now the king's men are here
I want to fight but Bess, Bess, Bess, never mind
'Fight,' said Bess, so I did
I killed, five, two more to go
'I win again,' I say
I lay in the hay
We lived forever, we didn't die, *great!*

Jessica Overhill (9)
St Peter's CE Primary School, Rochdale

The Highwayman
(Inspired by 'The Highwayman' by Alfred Noyes)

The wind was winding past the trees
The trees were blowing in the breeze
And the highwayman went galloping, galloping, galloping
The highwayman went galloping through the old creepy woods.

The trees were crooked and ancient
But as always the highwayman went galloping, galloping, galloping
The highwayman went galloping through the old creepy woods.

It was dreadful and miserable
The horse stopped and glared
The highwayman got frightened half to death

The horse had stopped because there were soldiers behind them
And so the highwayman didn't come galloping, galloping, galloping
The highwayman didn't go galloping through the old creepy woods.

Hannah Kelly (10)
St Peter's CE Primary School, Rochdale

The Highwayman
(Inspired by 'The Highwayman' by Alfred Noyes)

The highwayman came riding, riding, up the alley
Bess the landlord's daughter
The landlord's black-eyed daughter
Came walking up the alley.

The highwayman came riding, riding, riding
The redcoats looked to there, priming, priming, priming
She stood as still as a statue
As she saw him coming by and fainted with a sigh

With a good night's kiss and a trip on a horse
The highwayman came riding, riding, riding
The highwayman came riding up to the old inn door.

Saira Sattar (9)
St Peter's CE Primary School, Rochdale

Joy

Joy at having a holiday
Joy at playing on the beach
Joy of having a Galaxy chocolate cake
Joy at having a birthday
Joy at having a birthday at Camelot
Joy at going on all the rides
Joy at going to my favourite swimming pool
Joy of splashing all my friends
Joy at waking up on a crisp Christmas morning
Joy of ripping all my presents open
Joy of being the oldest cousin
Joy of seeing them on a Tuesday
Joy of seeing a koala bear
Joy of feeding it grass
Joy of the television
Joy of the television talking to me
Joy at getting my new DS games
Joy at playing on my new game (Hello Kitty)
Joy of listening to my iPod
Joy of listening to my favourite songs.

Rebecca Evitt (9)
Trinity & St Michael's CE School

Summer Fun

Summer brings us lots of fun
Summer brings us lots of sun
It is my favourite season of the year
It makes me jump up and cheer
Playing with my friends
I wish summer never ends
Making sand castles in the heat
Walking on the sand
Burning my feet.

Lewis Bennett-Holt (9)
Trinity & St Michael's CE School

Joy

Joy at playing on PlayStation 3 with my brother
Beating him 2-0 on Pro Evo 2009
Joy at playing basketball with my brother
In his room, probably losing 10-8
Joy of opening my birthday presents
Hoping to get a new Newcastle tracksuit
Joy at playing with my brother and sister
Hopefully beating them whatever we're playing
Joy of playing football, scoring a hat-trick
And winning 6-3 against Euxton Villa
Joy at sitting next to my aga when I'm cold
Whilst my mam runs me a nice warm bath
Joy of going to the Newcastle match
And going to the Chinese before the game
Joy of my dad cooking my favourite food
Chinese chicken with noodles or Moroccan lamb
Joy of getting presents at Christmas
Hoping to get PlayStation games.

Euan Stephenson (9)
Trinity & St Michael's CE School

Joy

Joy at opening my presents at Christmas
Joy at ripping my spotty paper off my present
Joy at getting new glasses
Joy at picking the colours that match
Joy at shopping with my sister
Joy at wearing the shiny clothes
Joy at picking blackberries with my sister
Joy at making blackberry crumble
Joy at going to the cattle auction
Joy at wearing my new overalls at the cattle auction
Joy at making chocolate cake with my sister
Joy at eating the chocolate cake after.

Jenny Gill (9)
Trinity & St Michael's CE School

Joy

The joy of noises from tiny kittens
The joy of touching that soft fur
The joy of breakfast in bed at the 5 star hotel
The joy of getting a suntan on the beach
The joy of playing on my Nintendo Wii, being a pro
The joy of beating my brother at baseball too
The joy of tearing wrappers on my Nintendo DS
The joy of seeing wrappers all over the place
The joy of building a snowman with a carrot nose
The joy of making snow angels with icy wings
The joy of chocolate, feel it melt in your mouth
The joy of Cadbury, Galaxy, Mars and Maltesers
The joy of getting into my goggles and costume
The joy of breaststroke, backstroke and splashing
The joy of X Factor and Britain's Got Talent
The joy of winners Diversity and Alexandra Burke.

Daisy Charlotte Sachs (9)
Trinity & St Michael's CE School

Joy

Joy at Christmas, receiving presents
Joy at looking inside the colourful presents
Joy at playing in the sun on the beach
Joy at sunbathing in the sun
Joy at watching SpongeBob
Joy at laughing at his funny jokes and him
Joy at hitting the ball in the hole playing golf
Joy at holding the club playing golf
Joy at the cinema, watching and eating
Joy at the cinema watching Wall-E
Joy on my birthday
Joy at eating the cake
Joy at drawing a picture
Joy at brushing the paintbrush.

Dylan Palmer (9)
Trinity & St Michael's CE School

Joy

Joy at the cold snowballs, throwing them about
Joy at getting people ice-cold wet
Joy at watching Most Haunted, looking at them scream
Joy at the places where they go to get their fiercest dreams
Joy at going on holiday at Center Parcs where it's fun
Joy at the woodland lodge where I am going
November the 6th on Friday after school
Joy at cute puppies, watching them play
Joy at their puppy dog face looking out of the window
Joy of cats and furry kittens running under a book or playing with
wool
Joy at them going on your bed and going to sleep
Joy of eating a chocolate bar, hearing it crunch
Joy of the taste that melts in your mouth.

Laura Hazeldine (9)
Trinity & St Michael's CE School

Joy Of

Joy of scoffing yummy chocolate
Joy of smelling the smell when you open the wrapper
Joy of opening my present on my birthday
Joy of eating the chocolate cake
Joy of watching the great TV
Joy of watching a really nice film
Joy of playing on the Wii
Joy of playing on FIFA '08
Joy of getting my pocket money
Joy of saving it up for a game
Joy of my friends when they comfort me
Joy of my friends when they play with me
Joy of my family when they care for me
Joy of my family when they take me on holiday.

Jayesh Shah (9)
Trinity & St Michael's CE School

Joy

Joy at watching my guinea pig run in her cage
Joy of stroking her soft, silky, white fur
Joy of the sleepover, having some fun
Joy of the pillow fight with everyone
Joy of my birthday, opening the presents
Joy of having a party and blowing out the candles
Joy of going to school every day
Joy of doing lots of work and getting praise
Joy of the dog running across the garden
Joy of him finding his favourite toy
Joy of summer, sitting under the warm sun
Joy of building really big sandcastles.

Bethany Charfe (9)
Trinity & St Michael's CE School

Joy

Joy of the dog chewing its toy
Joy of the dog running around
Joy of school doing lots of work
Joy of school chatting to friends
Joy of a sleepover having some fun
Joy of a pillow fight with everyone
Joy of my guinea pigs eating grass
Joy of stroking their smooth soft fur
Joy of the dog chasing my cat
Joy of the cat licking its kittens
Joy of summer eating ice cream
Joy of riding donkeys on the beach!

Shannon Buck (9)
Trinity & St Michael's CE School

Joy Of

Joy of watching a crab running around
Joy of a spider-like crab
Joy of watching a baby tortoise crawl around
Joy of watching them swim around
Joy of lizards and their funny colours
Joy of their funny faces
Joy of the little spiders
Joy of the little spindly legs
Joy of the little to large scorpions
Joy of the defensive sting
Joy of the snakes and their wonderful colours
Joy of their defensive bite.

Darcey Naylor (9)
Trinity & St Michael's CE School

Joy

Joy at riding through the thick long grass on my pony
Joy at racing my friends around the field
Joy of flying through the air on a plane at the start of my holiday
Joy of having a great time
Joy of the chocolate taste in my mouth
Joy of the texture of it melting in my mouth
Joy at the sound of people laughing on the beach
Joy at paddling my toes in the water
Joy of shopping through the street
Joy of trying on new clothes
Joy of waking up in the morning to find presents in my room
Joy of tearing off the paper that covers them up.

Antonia Urmson (10)
Trinity & St Michael's CE School

Joy

Joy at lying on the beach
Joy at watching the sea sway
Joy at Christmas, ripping open presents
Joy at sitting next to the fire
Joy of shopping, looking at clothes
Joy of shopping, looking through windows
Joy of chocolate, munching and crunching
Joy of the rich taste melting
Joy of swimming in the crystal pool
Joy of the chlorine drifting through the air
Joy of the fair, the exciting rides
Joy of the amazing rides up and down.

Caitlin Thompson (9)
Trinity & St Michael's CE School

Joy

Joy at receiving gifts on my birthday
Joy at ripping open the presents
Joy at playing in the sun
Joy at the warmth of sunny rays
Joy at scoring tries at rugby
Joy at all the wind going in my face
Joy at watching SpongeBob
Joy at laughing at all his funny jokes
Joy at the cinema watching Night At The Museum
Joy at Christmas ripping open my presents
Joy at looking at what I got.

Michael Hope (9)
Trinity & St Michael's CE School

Joy

Joy at the day when I buy more Lego
Joy at the sight of a beautifully made Lego model
Joy at the gleam of a newly bought crystal
Joy at the colour in front of the light
Joy at the night that seems forever
Joy at the darkness on a cold winter's day
Joy at hearing the comedy show
Joy at seeing my grandad smile when watching Last Of The Summer
Wine
Joy at my friends with all their smiles
Joy at all my friends with all their fun games.

Elliot Hicks (9)
Trinity & St Michael's CE School

Summer Holiday

Watching shows at the beach at night
In the pool when it's light
Summer brings so much sun
Lots of fun for everyone

Summer is my favourite season
Now everyone must have a reason
But unfortunately it has to end
So it's time to go and see its friend.

Anna Roscoe (9)
Trinity & St Michael's CE School

Summer Fun!

Summer, summer is so much fun
Summer, summer has just begun
Children playing on the beach
The warmth of the sand burns their feet
Ice cream, sunhats, glasses too
Bring a smile to me and you
Children shouting in the sea
Catching starfish, smiling with glee.

Kate Dalton (9)
Trinity & St Michael's CE School

Summertime

Summer brings us nice warm fun
To sunbathe and have summer fun
Children shouting from the sea
Seeing children licking ice creams
Catching crabs, collecting shells
Building castles, children's yells
Summer fun never ends, it only comes.

Imogen Stopforth (9)
Trinity & St Michael's CE School

Young Writers Information

We hope you have enjoyed reading this book - and that you will continue to enjoy it in the coming years.

If you like reading and writing poetry drop us a line, or give us a call, and we'll send you a free information pack.

Alternatively if you would like to order further copies of this book or any of our other titles, then please give us a call or log onto our website at www.youngwriters.co.uk.

Young Writers Information
Remus House
Coltsfoot Drive
Peterborough
PE2 9JX
(01733) 890066